DIAMOND
—IN THE—
ROUGH UNVEILED

BALDERES LUCILA SANTOS DE ALVAREZ

Order this book online at www.trafford.com
or email orders@trafford.com

Most Trafford titles are also available at major online book retailers.

Printed in the United States of America.

ISBN: 978-1-4669-9717-2 (sc)
ISBN: 978-1-4669-9719-6 (hc)
ISBN: 978-1-4669-9718-9 (e)

Library of Congress Control Number: 2013910645

Trafford rev. 07/31/2013

 www.trafford.com

North America & international
toll-free: 1 888 232 4444 (USA & Canada)
fax: 812 355 4082

The Ministry of Diamonds In The rough Unveiled is dedicated to Melody Nicole Cruz, whose passion has been to reach out to women of every walk of life; women who have been hurt by life's masquerades and hurt by poor choices, hurt by those who were meant to protect them, hurt by deceit, and women whose true beauty is yet to be unveiled. These women are "Diamonds In The Rough."

*****

I want to thank my friends, family and pastor for their contribution to this collection of thoughts. Thank you all for your prayers and support. I thank my husband, Armando R. Alvarez for helping me to stay focused and for encouraging me to move forward in obedience to my calling from God. I want to give special recognition to Edelweiss G. Santos Diaz for the translation of this book and Ciara Alexis Alvarez for the photography. I want to thank Bishop Austin Saughanto for telling me that I needed to stop playing ball in my backyard and start playing in the big league ball park. And so I begin!

Instructions:

This devotional book is meant to be used as a guide to enhance your meditation time with God's word. It is not intended to provide you with all the Spiritual nurture that you will require for your walk with God. It is a tool to be used in conjunction with your Bible reading time. It is structured in a way that will cause you to meditate on the Word of God and encourages you to use God's Word in your practical daily life. Use the note pages freely. There are no right or wrong answers. These are merely your thoughts, your prayers, your words. Use it as a journal, use it as a prayer book, use it to track how you are growing in your faith, use it to remember what God is doing in your life, use it memorize Scripture, use it however you like, just use it please.

Line your words up with God's word in agreement.

"These things we write, so that our joy may be made complete."
1 John 1:4

CONTENTS

Foreword

The renowned 16th century artist, Michaelangelo, is probably best known for his pain-staking renderings painted on the ceiling of Rome's Sistine Chapel. He is also recognized as the sculptor who created the near-flawless statue called "David." Of this sculpture, Michaelangelo is reported to have said, "I saw the angel in the marble and carved until I set him free."

In *Diamonds in the Rough* author, Balderes Alvarez suggests that God our Creator desires to "set free" diamonds hidden in rough stones. As the reader progresses through each entry, she is encouraged to allow God to carve away the rough stone that conceals her true self; the "self" uniquely designed by God. Alvarez offers Scripture, devotional readings and reflective questions to move the reader along in her spiritual transformation. She draws from real-life experiences and applies Biblical truths to everyday scenarios.

In the hands of the Divine Diamond Cutter the brilliance at the core of every daughter of God is further exposed. God sees the diamond in the stone and cuts until He sets it free. With a gentle hand Alvarez nudges the reader along as she yields to the artistry of her Maker.

"Now the Lord is the Spirit, and where the Spirit of the Lord is, there is freedom. And we all, who with unveiled faces contemplate the Lord's glory, are being transformed into his image with ever-increasing glory, which comes from the Lord, who is the Spirit" (2 Corinthians 3:17,18). Through Isaiah the Lord says, "you are precious and honored in my sight" (Isaiah 43:4a). In these pages Alvarez helps us uncover the precious gem God sees in us.

Major Alma Riley

WEEK 1/DAY ONE

Diamond in the Rough

The Urban Dictionary defines a Diamond in the Rough as "someone (or something) that has hidden exceptional characteristics and/or future potential, but currently lacks the final touches that would make them (or it) truly stand out from the crowd."

Have you ever felt less than adequate for the task? Carrying feelings of uncertainty while your shortcomings overpower your thoughts? All too often we limit ourselves from doing something God has extended to us as a gift, simply due to low self-esteem. Why not stop and take a look at yourself through the eyes of God? He sees us through Jesus Christ and sees us 'just as if we had never sinned.' He sees the beauty in us. He sees our potential. In His hands we can do remarkable things; far more things than we could possibly imagine. God is fascinated by you. Believe that!

(Psalm 45:11) Let the King be enthralled by your beauty; honor Him, for He is your Lord.

The Message Bible says it like this; 'the king is wild for you. Since he's your Lord, adore him.'

_____

_____

_____

_____

_____

_____

_____

DAY TWO

What characteristic of low self esteem do you possess? Galatians 5:22-23

_____

_____

_____

_____

_____

_____

DAY THREE

How do you think God sees you? Galatians 5:22-23

_____

_____

_____

_____

_____

_____

_____

DAY FOUR

What does "made in God's image" imply to you personally? Galatians 5:22-23

_____

_____

_____

_____

_____

_____

_____

DAY FIVE

What is beautiful about you? How can you enhance your spiritual beauty? Galatians5:22-23 & 1Peter1:15

_____

_____

_____

_____

_____

_____

_____

WEEK 2/DAY ONE

Get Out of the Boat

"If you are afraid to walk on water because of what people think, then you will never experience God and His promise for you and He will not become real to you, because a relationship without trust is not a relationship at all." Brown Charite

My husband invited me to go scuba diving with him one summer. I attempted to do so but was terribly distracted by the millions of crabs crawling on the very rocks where I had to walk to dive in. I could not get past that. My husband assured me that as I stepped forward the crabs would move. He instructed me to keep my eyes on him. I could not do it, so I missed out on the wonderful experience of the sea.

God has a wonderful experience waiting for you. Keep your eyes on Him, trust Him, step out of your comfort zone and He will direct your path.

Trust in the LORD with all your heart and lean not on your own understanding; in all your ways submit to Him, and He will make your paths straight. Proverbs 3:5,6

_____

_____

_____

_____

_____

_____

_____

DAY TWO

What do you need to do that requires a leap of faith? Will you do it? Hebrews 11:1 & 6

_____

_____

_____

_____

_____

_____

_____

DAY THREE

What are the storms in your life that keep you from completing your goal? Mark 4:35-41

_____

_____

_____

_____

_____

_____

_____

DAY FOUR

Pray for your pastor, that the Lord will protect him and his family and that He will place a hedge of protection around them. Hebrews 13:17-18

_____

_____

_____

_____

_____

_____

_____

DAY FIVE

How will you keep your eyes on Jesus and not be distracted by your circumstances? Mark 4:40

_____

_____

_____

_____

_____

_____

_____

WEEK 3/DAY ONE

A Father's Love

It seems as though the author of 1 John could no longer contain himself when he gets to chapter 3, he writes *"How great is the love the father has lavished on us, that we should be called children of God. And that is what we are!" (NIV)*

If truth be told, at times I do not feel this lavished love surrounding me because of sin in my life. I mess up; I forget God's commandments and my shortcomings get the best of me. At times I feel I have caused God's love for me to diminish, and He feels distant.

Several years ago my wife and I had the privilege of being the care givers for my 90 year old Dad. While this was a privilege, it was also challenging. My Dad had sworn off conventional medicine many years earlier, so trying to convince him to go to the doctor's office to get a checkup was challenging, at best. During this same time period, my Dad began to show signs of dementia; so the challenges of getting him to shower, eating at the right times, changing his clothes regularly keeping him from leaving the house at three in the morning, became part of our daily routine. As the dementia increased, my Dad became more stubborn and would not listen to me. One would think that the living out of this experience with my Dad would somehow diminish my love for him. On the contrary, my wife and I became more focused on helping him and we came up with all kinds of innovative ways to make his life more comfortable. Sometimes it worked, sometimes it didn't. In the midst of this turmoil, I noticed that my love for my Dad actually grew. Why? Because I loved him immensely and I was not focused on his actions, rather I was focused on the person my Dad had been all his life.

It occurs to me that at times I am stubborn. I do not always do what my Heavenly Father wants me to do. I do not always make the right choices in my life. And thus, I wonder if God still loves me. I have come to know that God's love and compassion for me actually increases during these times in my life. God is not focused on my actions, he is focused on the person I can be when he is allowed full reign in my life.

_____

_____

_____

_____

_____

_____

_____

<u>DAY TWO</u>

Do you ever feel as though you do not measure up to God's standard? Luke 15: 17-20

_____

_____

_____

_____

_____

_____

_____

DAY THREE

Are there recurring issues in your life that you desperately want God to take away or help you with? (1 John 1:9)

_____

_____

_____

_____

_____

_____

_____

DAY FOUR

Can God really identify with my weakness and still love me? Hebrews 4: 15-1

_____

_____

_____

_____

_____

_____

_____

DAY FIVE

How can I give God full reign in my life? Luke 1:27

_____

_____

_____

_____

_____

_____

_____

WEEK 4/DAY ONE

The Rising Sun

"From the rising of the sun to the going down of the same, the name of the Lord is praised."

The words of this chorus remind me of my need to rise up like the sun and praise my Lord with my first breath.

Will this day bring challenges? Will we have moments of difficulties? Will there be opportunity for us to be less than pleased with our circumstances, or the news we heard, or the treatment we received? Will there be interruptions? Probably! How 'bout in the middle of each un-welcomed situation we rise up and thank God for two things.

Example: Wi-Fi is not operating properly so I will not be able to continue my work . . . thank God because #1, I can take a well needed break and #2, I can take this moment to call my friend who really needs me and encourage her.

Romans 8:28, "And we know that all things work together for good to them that love God, to them who are the called according to His purpose."

As you rise today to take on the daily affairs of life, rise to the thought of God's love and take advantage of every interruption. Look out for these and praise your Lord!

_____

_____

_____

_____

_____

_____

_____

DAY TWO

What difficult situation did you have to deal with this week? How did you handle it? Matthew 11:28

_____

_____

_____

_____

_____

_____

DAY THREE

How will you trust God today to help you with your day? Matthew 21:2

_____

_____

_____

_____

_____

_____

DAY FOUR

What concern do you have that you still have not surrendered to the Lord? Will you surrender it now? James 4:8

_____

_____

_____

_____

_____

_____

_____

DAY FIVE

Who can you pray for that has very serious problems? Will you pray now? Psalm 61:1,2

_____

_____

_____

_____

_____

_____

_____

WEEK 5/DAY ONE

The Undetermined Future

"Indeed, how can people avoid what they don't know is going to happen?" Ecclesiastes 8:7

There is a reason why we do not know the future, why the future is a mystery to us. Perhaps it would cause us to make poor choices. Maybe it would limit us from doing good things. Possibly because we would go ahead of God and not live and learn the lessons set before us. Or perhaps we don't know the future so that we can rely upon God to guard our steps.

There are things we can do today to secure our tomorrow. There are many things that we can anticipate. Make good choices, yes! But, never lose sight of the fact that our future is in the hands of our loving God. Listen to Him with your heart and He will lead.

Jeremiah 29:11, "For I know the plans I have for you," declares the LORD, "plans to prosper you and not to harm you, plans to give you hope and a future."

_____

_____

_____

_____

_____

_____

DAY TWO

Since tomorrow is not promised, what can you do today to make a better tomorrow? Galatians 6:7-10

_____
_____
_____
_____
_____

DAY THREE

How much good can you do in one day? Galatians 6:9

_____
_____
_____
_____
_____
_____

DAY FOUR

How will you prepare for life today? Philippians 4:8

_____
_____
_____
_____
_____
_____

DAY FIVE

Often times our future sets us up in places where we have to react.
How will you know what to respond? Proverbs 4:7

_____

_____

_____

_____

_____

_____

_____

WEEK 6/DAY ONE

In His Time

Solomon says that God makes all things beautiful in His time. I don't always feel that way. Very often I feel that I have failed Him. I feel that I am sinful and ugly. I am deceived by the whispers of the enemy that tell me I will amount to nothing. Repeatedly my mind reminds me that I am not good and my thoughts revert to the poor choices I have made.

Has that ever happen to you? Have you struggled with thoughts of "I will never be good enough for God?" "How many times will I fail Him?"

In his song, Frank C says "how many times am I gonna sing to you before I ever change my ways and the things I do . . . ?" The Psalmist David felt that way too. In the songs he writes you can hear his heart cry out to God because of the way he has failed him. Despite this he is called "a man after God's own heart." (Acts 13:22)

In 1 Kings 14:8, God said David "followed me [God] with all his heart." The fact is that God continually works in our hearts to make us more like Jesus. And the great thing is that there is therefore now no condemnation for those who are in Christ Jesus, who walk not according to the flesh, but according to the Spirit . . . And He that searches the hearts knows . . . He knows your heart. (Romans 8)

_____

_____

_____

_____

_____

_____

_____

DAY TWO

Time will slip away quickly, how long will you lie there? Proverbs 6:9-11

_____

_____

_____

_____

_____

_____

_____

DAY THREE

What are you doing with the time God has given you? Proverbs 9:6

_____

_____

_____

_____

_____

_____

_____

DAY FOUR

What are your plans? Proverbs 12:5

_____

_____

_____

_____

_____

_____

_____

DAY FIVE

Start working on your goal today. Proverbs 14: 23

_____

_____

_____

_____

_____

_____

WEEK 7/DAY ONE

Love Eternal

"For love is as strong as death" (Song of Songs 8:6) Wow, what a comparison. I had to stop and think about this a minute because death comes with little pleasantries. Death sounds more like tragedy, sorrow and pain. However, death is strong, it is certain and permanent. Who can argue with death when it comes knocking? Who can change her mind when she calls? Who has the power to make her turn back?

What if we could love that way? The divorce rate may be lower. We would not have cause to war against our neighbors. Our kids would not bring guns to school. Teachers would be able to really teach. Our senior citizens would not die of loneliness and our churches would be filled with worshipers.

How much do you love? Will you keep on loving? Will you love even when it's not well received? Will your love be eternal? God's love is eternal and unchanging.

John 3:16 "For God so loved the world, that He gave his only begotten Son that whosoever believes in Him will not perish but have eternal life."

_____

_____

_____

_____

DAY TWO

Who do you know who appears to be in need of love? Ask God to bring to your remembrance someone to whom you can demonstrate love? Romans 5:8

_____

_____

_____

_____

_____

_____

DAY THREE

List three things that you can do right away to demonstrate your love for someone who really needs it. Luke 10:25-37

_____

_____

_____

_____

_____

_____

DAY FOUR

How can you love your enemy? Luke 6:27,28

_____

_____

_____

_____

_____

_____

_____

DAY FIVE

How do you compare to God's love? 1 John 3:1

_____

_____

_____

_____

_____

_____

_____

WEEK 8/DAY ONE

Show God Off

God is Love; love someone today

God is Patient; exercise patience with someone today

God is Kind; show kindness to your neighbor

God forgives; choose to forgive your enemy

God is compassionate; call someone you know who is hurting

God is merciful; forgive a debt

God is generous; give to a needy person

God is just; intervene on behalf of someone today

Look for an opportunity to show God off with your actions and others will want to follow.

Paul said in 1 Corinthians 11:1 "Imitate me, just as I also imitate Christ"

_____

_____

_____

_____

_____

_____

_____

DAY TWO

Proverbs 3:4, Job 10:12 What favor do you need from God?

_____

_____

_____

_____

_____

_____

DAY THREE

Psalm 84:11 How will you allow God to be your sun and shield?

_____

_____

_____

_____

_____

_____

DAY FOUR

Exodus 33:17 Do you know that God knows your name?

_____

_____

_____

_____

_____

_____

DAY FIVE

Psalm 115:12,13 Are you mindful of God's blessings?

_____

_____

_____

_____

_____

_____

WEEK 9/DAY ONE

Staying On Track

Charles Stanley spoke to my heart last night. On national TV he authorized listeners to take notes. Let me share some of that with you:

"How do I measure where I am in my walk with God?"

1- Schedule prayer and meditation in God's Word daily; Psalm 1:1-3 and Joshua 1
2- Obey God and leave all the consequences to Him; John 14:15,21,23
3- Trust God in every circumstances; Philippians 4
4- Wait upon the Lord for direction Isaiah 64:4
5- Give to God generously; "you can't out-give God." Luke 6:38

"If we know how to give, we will not be selfish, we will not be greedy, nor jealous. If we know how to give, we will not be covetous. Look at the cross and look at what God gave."

The first of this list gets me all the time. As soon as I lose hunger and thirst for his Word and my prayer time with Him, I know I am spiritually starving and I run back to my Heavenly Father.

Take some time each day and meditate on His love and His daily gifts.

_____

_____

_____

_____

_____

_____

_____

DAY TWO

Schedule prayer and meditation in God's Word daily; Psalm 1:1-3 and Joshua 1

_____

_____

_____

_____

_____

_____

DAY THREE

Obey God and leave all the consequences to Him; John 14:15,21,23

_____

_____

_____

_____

_____

_____

DAY FOUR

Trust God in every circumstances; Philippians 4

_____

_____

_____

_____

_____

_____

DAY FIVE

Wait upon the Lord for direction; Isaiah 64:4

_____

_____

_____

_____

_____

_____

WEEK 10/DAY ONE

His Love

My husband loves me so much. I know that because he demonstrates his love for me every day. He takes care of me and what is mine. If my car is dirty, he cleans it. If the wipers on my car are old, he replaces them. If I mess up my phone, he corrects it. He brings coffee to bed for me daily. He 'acts' like I'm beautiful even when I'm at my worst (big smile). He corrects me when I need correction in the kindest of ways. And he is careful to supply all of my needs. It's true! He really loves me.

What greater love does our Heavenly Father have for us?

When you are surrounded by a multitude of people who love you wholeheartedly, remember that this love is possible because God first loved us. When there is no human love in sight, remember God loves you just the way you are. When you begin to contemplate on the idea that YOU love God consider the fact that HE loved you before you even had the thought to love Him.

1 John 3:1 How great is the love the Father has lavished on us, that we should be called children of God!

_____

_____

_____

_____

_____

_____

_____

DAY TWO

John 3:16 Meditate on the awesomeness of this truth.

_____

_____

_____

_____

_____

_____

_____

DAY THREE

1 John 4:7-12 What would happen if we loved each other?

_____

_____

_____

_____

_____

_____

_____

DAY FOUR

Jeremiah 31:3 Consider the love of your Lord!

_____

_____

_____

_____

_____

_____

_____

DAY FIVE

Ephesians 3:17-19 What if we really believe that God loves us?

_____

_____

_____

_____

_____

_____

_____

WEEK 11/DAY ONE

Like Clay In The Hand of The Potter

[1] This is the word that came to Jeremiah from the LORD: [2] "Go down to the potter's house, and there I will give you my message." [3] So I went down to the potter's house, and I saw him working at the wheel. [4] But the pot he was shaping from the clay was **marred** in his hands; so the potter formed it into another pot, shaping it as seemed best to him. Jeremiah18:1-6

[5] Then the word of the LORD came to me. [6] He said, "Can I not do with you,_____(Israel), as this potter does?" declares

Your Name Here

the LORD. "Like clay in the hand of the potter, so are you in my hand,_____(Israel).

Your Name Here

To be "marred" means to detract from the perfection or wholeness of; spoil

Five things the potter is doing:

1. He is at work at the wheel
2. He is shaping (to make fit for as a particular use or purpose)
3. He is forming (to model by instruction and discipline)
4. He is not giving up on the clay
5. He is looking out for the best interest of the clay

Things to ponder on . . . . .

1. How do we know that The Potter is at work in us? How does it feel?
2. Describe a moment when you felt like God wasn't at work?
3. Consider the difference between forming and shaping? How does it feel when the Potter does this?

_____

_____

_____

_____

_____

_____

_____

DAY TWO

How does the world view "marred" clay? How does The Potter view "marred" clay? Isaiah 59:15-17

_____

_____

_____

_____

_____

_____

_____

DAY THREE

Describe how it feels to know the way The Lord views us? Isaiah 64:8

_____

_____

_____

_____

_____

_____

_____

DAY FOUR

Once the marred clay is formed and shaped again, can it become marred again? How does The Potter respond? Psalm 31:12

_____

_____

_____

_____

_____

_____

_____

DAY FIVE

Is there a ministry you feel God is shaping you for? Romans 8:1-15

_____

_____

_____

_____

_____

_____

WEEK 12/DAY ONE

Starting Your Day Right

As soon as you open your eyes and you realize you have been gifted with a new day . . . take a deep breath . . . pause for a moment and thank God that He allowed you to wake up. Think of one positive thing in your life and acknowledge it. For example, "thank God for my warm blanket."

Wash up and if possible, (even if it is through your window) recognize God's glory in the air, in the clouds, in the trees. Tell Him that you appreciate the gift of His creation . . . like this "Lord, thank you for the wind blowing the leaves of trees, they remind me to praise you."

You dressed? Now take a moment and to open your Bible and read one or two verses. Ponder the words you read and Thank God for the freedom you have to read them. Here you go:

Psalm 139:13 "You made all the delicate, inner parts of my body and knit me together in my mother's womb."

How big is that miracle? Does He know the real you? Does He know your body? Can He handle your situation? Can He heal? Does He love you, His creation? Think on His Word!

_____
_____
_____
_____
_____

DAY TWO

Psalm 50:1-6 Worship Him today

_____
_____
_____
_____
_____
_____

DAY THREE

Psalm 101 Consecrate yourself to Him today

_____
_____
_____
_____
_____
_____

DAY FOUR

Psalm 108 Praise Him today

_____

_____

_____

_____

_____

_____

DAY FIVE

Psalm 128 Trust Him today

_____

_____

_____

_____

_____

_____

_____

WEEK 13/DAY ONE

Omnipotent Father

Song: Written by Melody Nicole Cruz

Omnipotent Father, Creator of all; My Lord, My Savior, My All

Omnipotent Father, Creator of all; My Strength, My Fortress, My Whole.

I lift my hands to adore you; I close my eyes to meditate on you;

I bow on my knees to serve you Heavenly Father; Oh, how I long to live for you; Lord, I want to live for you. Genesis 17:1

_____

_____

_____

_____

_____

_____

_____

DAY TWO

Omnipotent Father, Creator of all; My God, My Redeemer, My Joy

Omnipotent Father, Creator of all; My Life, My Spirit, My Song.

My Answer, My Provider, My Faith.

I clap my hands to praise you I cry out loud to exalt your Holy name

I kneel on my knees to give you all the glory; Oh how I long to live for you

Lord, How I want to live for you. Psalm 84:12

_____

_____

_____

_____

_____

_____

_____

DAY THREE

Omnipotent Father, Creator of all; The Son, The Lamb, My Gift

Omnipotent Father, Creator of all; My Spirit, My best friend, My Peace

I lay on my face to humble. I sing your name to show I testify; I fall on my knees to worship you wonderful Master; Oh, how I long to live for you; Lord, I want to live for you. Psalm 91:1

_____

_____

_____

_____

_____

_____

_____

DAY FOUR

Omnipotent Father, Creator of all; My Heart, My keeper, My fire

Omnipotent Father, Creator of all; My king, My loved one, My Soul

My Potter, My Deliverer, My Way.

Omnipotent Father, Creator of all; You died, You saved me, the Lamb

Omnipotent Father, Creator of all; You cleansed me, restored me, my rest. Isaiah 5:16

_____

_____

_____

_____

_____

_____

_____

DAY FIVE

Write your own words. Philippians 2:9-11

_____

_____

_____

_____

_____

_____

_____

WEEK 14/DAY ONE

Radically Obedient

Hebrews 11:7 By faith Noah, when warned about things not yet seen, in holy fear built an ark to save his family. By his faith he condemned the world and became heir of the righteousness that is in keeping with faith.

Noah had no visible sign of rain, yet he trusted that God would keep His Word.

There are numerous promises that God has made to His obedient children even to you personally. Be radical, obey God! While obedience to God may not seem popular these days and most people around you will ridicule you, still trust and obey Him.

Take time to number the promises that God has made to you and focus on those today. Remember that although things may not look quite clear, He will keep his word to you as He did with Noah.

_____
_____
_____
_____
_____
_____
_____

DAY TWO

What rewards are you working for? Matthew 16:27

_____

_____

_____

_____

_____

_____

_____

DAY THREE

What kind of freedom are you reaching for? John 8:31-32

_____

_____

_____

_____

_____

_____

_____

DAY FOUR

What kind of love do you long for? John 14:21,23

_____

_____

_____

_____

_____

_____

_____

DAY FIVE

What blessings are you living for? James 1:25

_____

_____

_____

_____

_____

_____

WEEK 15/DAY ONE

The House of The Lord

How lovely is your dwelling place, LORD Almighty! My soul yearns, even faints, for the courts of the LORD; my heart and my flesh cry out for the living God. Even the sparrow has found a home, and the swallow a nest for herself, where she may have her young—a place near your altar, LORD Almighty, my King and my God. Blessed are those who dwell in your house; they are ever praising you. Psalm 84:1-4

My church is being remodeled. We have expanded the location because we have grown in number. I have the privilege of decorating and adding plants and chairs and giving suggestions for the transformation of the building and I get excited about it.

I love the house of God and in particular the one He has assigned to me. Within those walls I have seen lives changed, broken marriages mended, children healed, prayers answered and souls renewed, revived. I have experienced God's presence in this place and it has been powerful.

Like the Psalmist, I too love to be in the house where the Lord dwells.

_____
_____
_____
_____

_____

_____

_____

DAY TWO

What motivates you to spend time in the house of the Lord? Psalm 84:10

_____

_____

_____

_____

_____

_____

DAY THREE

What can you do in your church to make it more welcoming? Psalm 133:1

_____

_____

_____

_____

_____

_____

DAY FOUR

How will you contribute to the worship of God in your church? Psalm 66

_____

_____

_____

_____

_____

_____

DAY FIVE

What can you share in an effort to demonstrate your love? Acts 4:32

_____

_____

_____

_____

_____

_____

WEEK 16/DAY ONE

If I Never Feel a Thing

"I believe, help Thou my unbelief, I take the finite risk of trusting like a child." Bill Gaither sings this song. He goes on, "I walk into the unknown" . . . . still trusting. The songs describes others feeling something special but the desire of the author is "should I never feel a thing, I claim Him [Jesus] even so."

The author of Proverbs advises us to trust in the Lord with all our heart and not to lean on our own understanding . . . The Message Bible says it this way: "Trust GOD from the bottom of your heart; don't try to figure out everything on your own. Listen for GOD's voice in everything you do, everywhere you go; he's the one who will keep you on track."

There are times in our lives when we feel the Lord very near and we are excited, but other times we simply need to trust Him blindly, whether we feel it or not. Let's not lean on our own understanding or on what we see nor what we feel, instead, if we should never feel a thing, still trust Him and claim Him even so."

_____

_____

_____

_____

_____

DAY TWO

Matthew 6:28-30 What are you feeling or NOT feeling?

_____

_____

_____

_____

_____

_____

_____

DAY THREE

Luke 12:22-29 How can flowers remind you of what you know about God?

_____

_____

_____

_____

_____

_____

_____

DAY FOUR

Isaiah 26:4 Can you recognize God's greatness despite what you feel?

_____

_____

_____

_____

_____

_____

_____

DAY FIVE

How does Abraham encourage your faith? Romans 4:18-21

_____

_____

_____

_____

_____

_____

_____

WEEK 17/DAY ONE

Sometimes I Cry

Jason Crabb sings this song that was written by his dad called "Sometimes I Cry." It's a song that moves me because I too "look the part and blend in with the rest of the church crowd" like the song says. I teach a Bible study and watch Christian TV . . . I've "been born again, and without a doubt I know I'm saved" and on my way to eternal life in heaven with my Savior Jesus . . .

"But sometimes I hurt and sometimes I cry." There are times that I just don't get it all right. I really try hard and still "sometimes I fall down." But I get up again and again and again because we are "struck down but not destroyed." 2 Corinthians 4:8,9

_____

_____

_____

_____

_____

_____

_____

DAY TWO

Where does your strength come from? 2 Corinthians 4:7

_____

_____

_____

_____

_____

_____

_____

DAY THREE

Who do you call on in your distress? Psalm 120

_____

_____

_____

_____

_____

_____

_____

DAY FOUR

Where does your help come from? Psalm 121

_____

_____

_____

_____

_____

_____

_____

DAY FIVE

Isaiah 43:1-3 What trouble is too big for God?

_____

_____

_____

_____

_____

_____

_____

WEEK 18/DAY ONE

My Homeland

"Do not be conformed to this world, but be transformed by the renewing of your mind." Romans 12:2

It is so hard to imagine a world greater than our own, maybe that's why this transformation is so difficult . . . . So challenging to conform myself to the identity of a citizen in my home land . . . my Kingdom! And I wonder how many of us choose to deny that there is anything beyond this world to be convinced that no change is needed . . . that we are just fine how and where we are? Sacrificing transformation into our Royal Priesthood, never taking rightful place as heirs to the throne in our Father's kingdom.

Revelation says that on 'judgment day' there will be weeping and gnashing of teeth, I wonder if those tears will be shed because God will show us everything that he had planned for us here on earth . . . . all the things that we did not take hold of, or do for our Father's Kingdom . . . because we refused to be transformed?

Written by Priscilla Cruz

_____

_____

_____

_____

_____
_____
_____

DAY TWO

What does your house look like? John 14:1-4

_____
_____
_____
_____
_____
_____
_____

DAY THREE

Where is your treasure? Matthew 6:19-24

_____
_____
_____
_____
_____
_____
_____

DAY FOUR

What is your heart and mind set on? Colossians 3:1,2 &16,17

_____

_____

_____

_____

_____

_____

_____

DAY FIVE

Luke 12:34 Have you thought this through? Where is your treasure?

_____

_____

_____

_____

_____

_____

_____

WEEK 19/DAY ONE

To See or Not to See

God's word tells us about a man named Bartimeus, who was seeking healing from his blindness. While Bartimeus' blindness was physical, we may be experiencing spiritual blindness. While we know that God blesses us, it is possible that we don't always see all that He really does, moment by moment, so we can become ungrateful. We don't see what His plans are for us, so we try to do things ourselves. We also fail to see our faults and sins. Sometimes we would rather be blind to these and not take responsibility for what we do, say, think or feel, keeping us from being repentant. Something else that we may be blind to is the needs of others, so we fail to follow God's commandment to love our neighbors as ourselves. Once we recognize our blindness, we must do as Bartimeus did and cry out to Jesus to receive His glorious gift of light.

There is something very significant that Bartimeus did in answer to Jesus' call . . . he left his garments behind. There are an untold number of things that we are each individually bound to; only you know what those are in your own life. These may be fears, desires of the flesh, the opinions of others, procrastination, laziness, etc. Just as Bartimeus did, it is imperative that we leave these "garments" behind.

As Bartimeus searched for healing from Jesus, there were voices telling him to be quiet. In a spiritual way, there are voices keeping us from calling on Jesus. Maybe the voices are saying, "He won't listen to you";

"You're not good enough"; "Things are fine the way they are"; "He's going to require something of you"; "It's too hard to change." These voices may really be saying that you lack faith and trust. The way Bartimeus quieted the voices which were telling him to stop calling on Jesus was by calling even more, and even louder. We ought to follow suit and call above the sound of those negative voices. The result will be that our Lord will listen and respond to our cry. When He asks us what we want, let's be ready to make our request known to Him. We want spiritual sight . . . then, as Bartimeus did, we won't simply go on our way, but we'll follow closely behind Jesus.

DAY TWO

How can we be sure that we have received His glorious gift of light? 2 Corinthians 4:6

DAY THREE

Are there cloaks that you and I need to leave behind? Hebrews 12:1

_____

_____

_____

_____

_____

_____

DAY FOUR

Whose voice should we be listening to? John 10:27

_____

_____

_____

_____

_____

_____

DAY FIVE

What happens when we follow close to Jesus? John 8:12

_____

_____

_____

_____

_____

_____

WEEK 20/DAY ONE

Insecurities

Stressed about a particular situation in your life? Have you become anxious about something you fear may happen or of something that you were counting on, but has not come through yet? Maybe it is even finding out about the condition of your health or that of a loved one and it has become close to unbearable? Brothers and Sisters, God knew we would face these uncertainties and emotional challenging situations. He knew about our insecurities and fears and our limitations. He drew a map for us to journey into relief and rest in Him when He wrote: "Do not be anxious about anything, but in everything, by prayer and petition, with thanksgiving, present your requests to God."(Phil 4:6) Did you read that? Wow! God is saying, don't worry about something that only I can do, just come and talk to me about it. Jesus says, Don't hold it in, don't explode, don't stress it. Just share it with me.

_____
_____
_____
_____
_____
_____
_____

DAY TWO

Whom do you trust? Psalm 9:10

_____

_____

_____

_____

_____

_____

_____

DAY THREE

Who is your Lord? Psalm 94:14

_____

_____

_____

_____

_____

_____

_____

DAY FOUR

Who is your Father and Mother? Psalm 27:10

_____

_____

_____

_____

_____

_____

_____

DAY FIVE

Who will you count on even unto the end of the world? Matthew 28:20

_____

_____

_____

_____

_____

_____

_____

WEEK 21/DAY ONE

Your Own Personal Trainer

In the 90's Oprah Winfrey lost more than 100 pounds and ran the Marine Corps Marathon in 1994. She finished in four hours and 29 minutes which was an average time. This was the first drastic weight loss feat that viewers witnessed her accomplish. Now, almost ten years later we've also witnessed her gain and lose and gain and lose multiple times. These days she graces the cover of her *O Magazine* and seems to have finally settled into her maintenance weight.

Yet back in the 90's many wondered, much like I did, how in the world she accomplished such a feat. Her secret? His name was Bob Greene, Oprah's personal trainer. We all watched and thought, "If I had a personal trainer with me every day, I could do that too." So here's a critical element in our spiritual training; a personal trainer. Now here's the good news, we have access to our own personal trainer; the Holy Spirit. John 14:26 refers to Him as our teacher. In John 16:13 He's described as our guide and Romans 8:26 says He's our helper. And what makes Him unlike any other is that He runs the course with us and if we should fall, He picks us up and carries us. Thank God, we don't have to go into training alone. His very presence is with us daily allowing us to declare, "I press on to reach the end of the race and receive the heavenly prize for which God, through Christ Jesus, is calling us" (Philippians 3:14) and. "I can do all things through Christ who strengthens me" (Philippians 4:13).

_____

_____

_____

_____

_____

_____

_____

_____

DAY TWO

In what areas of your life do you know you need to cut out the spiritual fat? 1 Corinthians 9:25

_____

_____

_____

_____

_____

_____

DAY THREE

Reflect on what things might be getting in the way of you giving control of your training over to the Holy Spirit. Hosea 7:15

_____

_____

_____

_____

_____

_____

_____

DAY FOUR

Compose a personal prayer and enlist the help of the Holy Spirit as you start your new training program. Luke 6:40

_____

_____

_____

_____

_____

_____

DAY FIVE

2 Samuel 22:35 What training do your hands need?

_____

_____

_____

_____

_____

_____

WEEK 22/DAY ONE

Without Words

There are pleasant surprises, but also other unpleasant ones. There is good news and bad. The common response to bad news is "No, it can't be!" Sometimes we spend days, maybe weeks denying the news and perhaps praying that it's not true, then the day of confirmation comes. At that time it is common to be speechless.

Many times there are no words to express the astonishment, sadness or surprise. In moments where the news is bad, and we have already received confirmation we have a promise in the Bible that gives us hope.

So when we run out of words and when we don't know what to say, how to ask, the Spirit speaks on our behalf. Romans 8:26 In the same way, the Spirit helps us in our weakness. We do not know what we ought to pray for, but the Spirit himself intercedes for us with groans that words cannot express."

_____

_____

_____

_____

_____

_____

_____

DAY TWO

What has been the greatest news that has left you speechless? 1 Peter 5:7

_____

_____

_____

_____

_____

_____

_____

DAY THREE

How do you compare the intensity of your surprise with the way the Spirit intercedes on your behalf? Ro. 8:26-27

_____

_____

_____

_____

_____

_____

_____

DAY FOUR

How does Romans 8:28 encourage you?

_____

_____

_____

_____

_____

_____

_____

DAY FIVE

What news is too difficult for our God? Romans 8:31

_____

_____

_____

_____

_____

_____

_____

WEEK 23/DAY ONE

Discipline

Nobody likes Discipline, but undisciplined children are spoiled . . . undisciplined adults are damaged goods.

Nobody likes Discipline, but without it we would not learn how to conduct ourselves properly because our tendency is self-centeredness.

Nobody likes Discipline, because it hurts and we don't want to feel pain or suffering, but without discipline we would not appreciate the health and blessings that we have.

Nobody likes Discipline, but it is what produces life and Holiness, justice and peace because the Lord disciplines those whom He loves.

_____

_____

_____

_____

_____

_____

_____

DAY TWO

Is punishment and discipline considered as one and the same? Hebrews 12: 3-11

_____

_____

_____

_____

_____

_____

_____

DAY THREE

In your opinion, according to Proverbs 29:15, what does 'discipline' represent?

_____

_____

_____

_____

_____

_____

_____

DAY FOUR

What does enduring hardship mean to you? Hebrews 12:7

_____

_____

_____

_____

_____

_____

_____

DAY FIVE

Proverbs 3:11 encourages us to welcome the discipline of the Lord, will you?

_____

_____

_____

_____

_____

_____

_____

WEEK 24/DAY ONE

<u>Great Things</u>

"Many great things can be done in a day if you don't make that day tomorrow" (unknown). Lord, please free me from yesterday's fears and worries so that I can make the very best of today. Psalm 23

_____

_____

_____

_____

_____

_____

DAY TWO

How often do you leave for tomorrow what you can do today? Proverbs 30:25

_____

_____

_____

_____

_____

_____

DAY THREE

What part does laziness play in your life? Proverbs 10:4

_____

_____

_____

_____

_____

_____

DAY FOUR

What are you doing with your talent? Matthew 25:26

_____

_____

_____

_____

_____

_____

DAY FIVE

What rewards will your diligence bring you? Hebrews 11:6

_____

_____

_____

_____

_____

_____

WEEK 25/DAY ONE

Nature Declares His Glory

Yesterday my daughter and I sat by the Canal in front of our apartment. To the right of us were two bald eagles in their nest chattering. Across the water was a raccoon fishing. Then one by one three sea otters came bouncing down the embankment and into the water swimming downstream. I love these moments when we can enjoy the works of God in all His Majesty. Such experiences should always be treasured.

_____

_____

_____

_____

_____

_____

_____

DAY TWO

How often do you recognize God's creation around you and give thanks? Genesis 1

_____

_____

_____

_____

_____

_____

_____

DAY THREE

Can you think of two ways that you can exalt God today? Psalm 8

_____

_____

_____

_____

_____

_____

_____

DAY FOUR

Take a moment to meditate on God's greatness. Job 38

_____

_____

_____

_____

_____

_____

_____

DAY FIVE

Look to the heavens and see God's glory. Psalm 19:1

_____

_____

_____

_____

_____

_____

_____

WEEK 26/DAY ONE

In The Midst of Trials

As Christians, we know that we have an enemy that wants to dominate us and wars against us so that we might be defeated, fall prostrate at his feet and submit to him. When in the midst of trials and tribulations if we remain firmly grounded in Christ and we reverence our Lord in obedience, even in the middle of difficult circumstances and persecution we will be rewarded by God.

Many are the men and women whom for the sake of Jesus Christ endured great hardship. A Biblical example is the Apostle Paul. After his conversion he preached the message of Jesus Christ and became a target for persecution. He was eventually arrested in Jerusalem on charges of bringing Greeks into the Temple; he was imprisoned in Caesarea for two years. After he appealed his case to the emperor he was sent to Rome. In Rome he was placed under house arrest for two years. His death is not recorded in the Bible although later traditions say that he was martyred.

The author of the book of Hebrews mentions the suffering of many. Starting in verse thirty six, the author references the forefathers of Christianity and says, " . . . some faced jeers and flogging, and even chains and imprisonment. They were put to death by stoning; they were sawed in two; they were killed by the sword. They went about in sheepskins and goatskins, destitute, persecuted and mistreated;

the world was not worthy of them. They wandered in deserts and mountains, living in caves and in holes in the ground.

Jesus Himself said, "Remember what I told you: 'A servant is not greater than his master.' If they persecuted me, they will persecute you also. If they obeyed my teaching, they will obey yours also." John 15:20

Meditate on this: "In all this you greatly rejoice, though now for a little while you may have had to suffer grief in all kinds of trials. 7 These have come so that the proven genuineness of your faith—of greater worth than gold, which perishes even though refined by fire—may result in praise, glory and honor when Jesus Christ is revealed. 8 Though you have not seen him, you love him; and even though you do not see him now, you believe in him and are filled with an inexpressible and glorious joy, 9 for you are receiving the end result of your faith, the salvation of your souls." 1 Peter 1:6-9

_____

_____

_____

_____

_____

_____

_____

DAY TWO

Are you exempt from afflictions? John 16:33

_____

_____

_____

_____

_____

_____

_____

DAY THREE

What will you do in the midst of temptation? James 4:7

_____

_____

_____

_____

_____

_____

DAY FOUR

How will you respond to trials? Psalm 100:4,5

_____

_____

_____

_____

_____

_____

DAY FIVE

What will my reward be? James 1:12

_____

_____

_____

_____

_____

_____

_____

WEEK 27/DAY ONE

Financial Advise

"The love of money is the root of all evil." 1 Timothy 6:10. YET, **we all need money** to live so we work for it and rightly so. Money itself is not evil. Without money we cannot buy food, clothing, shoes or pay for a place to live. Our society is structured in a way that one without money would die. Jesus said "give to Caesar what is Caesar's, and to god what is God's." (Matthew 22:21). There is a separation of the two. I choose to give God number one place in my life because He owns the cattle on a thousand hills and He loves to share with me. The author of Hebrews 13:5 says "keep your lives free from the love of money and be content with what you have, because God has said, never will I leave you; never will I forsake you." That's a promise to provide for us. He loves to give to His children. Love God above all; use money wisely.

_____

_____

_____

_____

_____

_____

_____

DAY TWO

Malachi 3:6-12 Test God in this! **Plan to give**

_____

_____

_____

_____

_____

_____

DAY THREE

Proverbs 6:6-8 See the Ant **Plan to save**

_____

_____

_____

_____

_____

_____

DAY FOUR

The borrower is servant to the lender: Proverbs 22:7b **Plan to pay back**

_____

_____

_____

_____

_____

_____

DAY FIVE

List what you can do to improve your finances a bit.

_____

_____

_____

_____

_____

_____

_____

WEEK 28/DAY ONE

Would I Survive?

I have seen days of great fear, days that felt so long, dark and hard that I wasn't sure if I would survive. Days where I saw everything crumbling down upon me, days where I saw no light. Days that promised no way out. My body became ill and my nights filled with tears and trembling.

But everyday loud and clear God spoke to me and let me know that He was holding on to me. He was calling out to me "I have you, I have you, you're in my arms."

Thanks be to God that He still saves . . . even today. Psalm 56:3 & 4

Written 10/14/2005

_____

_____

_____

_____

_____

_____

_____

DAY TWO

Psalm 40:1-3 How long can you wait on God?

_____

_____

_____

_____

_____

_____

DAY THREE

Why all of this? 2 Corinthians 1:9,10

_____

_____

_____

_____

_____

_____

DAY FOUR

Here's a gift The Lord gives you. John 14:27

_____

_____

_____

_____

_____

_____

DAY FIVE

Make Scripture yours today. Psalm 2:8—Psalm 3:4—Psalm 4:1—Psalm 5:7&8

_____

_____

_____

_____

_____

_____

_____

WEEK 29/DAY ONE

Attitude

"Go up to the top of Pisgah and look west and north and south and east. Look at the land with your own eyes, since you are not going to cross this Jordan. But commission Joshua, and encourage and strengthen him,"(Deut3:27-28).

God had big plans and big dreams for Moses. God promised him His provision and His support. God, on several occasions, moved on Moses' prayers. Moses was a godly man. He even spoke to God face to face(Ex33:11). But Moses' attitude got the best of him. His attitude impede him from reaching his God given plan. His attitude was revealed when people pushed the right buttons. And because of it, he went only as far as seeing what he should have lived in. He dreamed of a place, that he was never able to reach, because he had an attitude problem. Not always will a potential job or ministry give you an opportunity because of skills that you do have; they will often look at your attitude. Be a team player, approachable, graceful, wise, patient; ask God to help you cultivate a good attitude, and reach your potential.

_____

_____

_____

_____

_____

_____

_____

DAY TWO

Joshua 24:15 What will you let go of?

_____

_____

_____

_____

_____

_____

DAY THREE

Exodus 20:12 Who do you need to honor?

_____

_____

_____

_____

_____

_____

_____

DAY FOUR

Psalms 127:3-5 What will make you happy today?

_____
_____
_____
_____
_____
_____
_____

DAY FIVE

Deuteronomy 6:6-9 How important is the Word of God? Will you let
it impact your attitude?

_____
_____
_____
_____
_____
_____
_____

WEEK 30/DAY ONE

What Did He Say?

On January 25, 2009 I heard a message from Bishop Saughanto who said that we have ignored God. He impressed on his listeners the importance of staying in touch with God through His Word. He quoted 2 Timothy 2:15 that instructs us to study the Word so as to show ourselves approved, a workman, a laborer—laboring in the Word; One who does not need to be ashamed and who correctly handles the Word of truth. He said, "one Psalm a day won't keep the doctor away."

There are times when I study the Word so that I am prepared to teach others and I miss what God wants to say to me personally.

So, how do we do this? We start by inviting the Holy Spirit to enlighten us. We go to weekly Bible study class. We attend Sunday school. We join a home study group. We use a good devotional book that motivates us to read the Word further. We take notes and read on, ask questions, take more notes, read further. We study and then we leave the rest to the Holy Spirit.

_____

_____

_____

_____

_____

_____

DAY TWO

Hosea 4:6 What holds you back from studying His Word?

_____

_____

_____

_____

_____

_____

DAY THREE

James 1:22 What will you do with the Word you receive?

_____

_____

_____

_____

_____

_____

DAY FOUR

James 2:17 What does this Scripture mean to you?

_____

_____

_____

_____

_____

_____

<u>DAY FIVE</u>

Philippians 2:12 Where does this Scripture take you in your walk with
Jesus?

_____

_____

_____

_____

_____

_____

_____

WEEK 31/DAY ONE

Reward Focused

I don't really follow basketball, but I was struck by a comment that my husband said about Carmelo Anthony from the Knicks. Apparently at the start of this season he was doing much better than last season. According to Suri (my husband) the difference is last season the players were on strike and during that time he gained weight and was therefore, not on his game. This time around he is slimmer and is showing his worth more so. I started to think about the fact that when athletes are disciplined they have to give up a lot of things such as eating whatever they want and doing whatever they want with their time—you have to eat right, exercise, practice etc. But when an athlete is disciplined the reward is worth it in the end. As humans we have a tendency to be more focused on what we are going to lose if we give our lives to God, but that will only lead us to miss out on the rewards at the end (peace, joy, meaningful life, truly helping others and so much more).

The Knicks paid a lot of money to have Carmelo win games because they know his worth, but he may have not shown his fullest potential due to a lack of discipline. Jesus paid even more for us on the cross because he knows our worth and I am challenged by the fact that there could be more victories in my life that I have not obtained due to my lack of discipline (lack of consistent praying, reading the Word, fasting, etc). However, as I write this, a new year is upon us and I believe this season will be better than the last.

". . . let us lay aside every weight, and the sin which so easily ensnares us, and let us run with endurance the race that is set before us, looking unto Jesus, the author and finisher of our faith, who for the joy that was set before Him endured the cross, despising the shame, and has sat down at the right hand of the throne of God." (Hebrews 12:1-2).

Jesus was able to endure the pain of the cross, because he focused on the joy of seeing us saved and reconciled to God the Father.

Pray, read the Bible, go to church

_____

_____

_____

_____

_____

_____

DAY TWO

What can happen if you focus on what you will gain with God, not what you will lose out on?

_____

_____

_____

_____

_____

_____

DAY THREE

What exercise will it take to equip you for this Spiritual race? Ephesians 6:10-20

_____

_____

_____

_____

_____

_____

_____

DAY FOUR

Philippians 2:13 How will you actively move in the direction where God is leading you?

_____

_____

_____

_____

_____

_____

_____

<u>DAY FIVE</u>

What's your "work-out" plan for today? Philippians 2:12

_____

_____

_____

_____

_____

_____

_____

WEEK 32/DAY ONE

Rise up!

Yet still I rise. Never to give up, Never to give in against all odds

Yet still I rise. High above the clouds, At times I feel Low

Above all my problems. Above all my fears. Above all my eyes can see
Knowing God is able to strengthen me. Yet still I rise.

Song by Yolanda Adams

Daily I ask God to grant me the strength to rise up again. Though
many challenges and disappointments may lie ahead of me, still I
remember that it is the Lord Jesus who is by my side. He gives me
what it takes to make it through. He shows me the great things He has
already done and helps me to focus on those rather than the enemy's
lies. I can never go so low that my Jesus won't reach me. He is right
where you are right now. Rise up and never give up!

_____

_____

_____

_____

_____

_____

_____

DAY TWO

Deuteronomy 31:6 Where can you go that Jesus will leave you or forsake you?

_____

_____

_____

_____

_____

_____

DAY THREE

1 John 4:4 Whose word will you believe today?

_____

_____

_____

_____

_____

_____

DAY FOUR

2 Thessalonians 2:15-17 How will you stand firm?

_____

_____

_____

_____

_____

_____

_____

DAY FIVE

Romans 8:35 Who can separate you from the Love of God?

_____

_____

_____

_____

_____

_____

WEEK 33/DAY ONE

Sweet Gathering

Someone once said that when a piece of coal burns on its own it will die out much more quickly than if coal is together with other pieces of coal. I would imagine that if you keep throwing more coal on a pile of burning coal that it would never stop burning. One reason why Thomas, Jesus' disciple, doubted Christ's resurrection is because he was not gathered with the group of believers at His appearance. John 20:24 "Now Thomas one of the Twelve, was not with the disciples when Jesus came." The author of Hebrews encourages us to gather with fellow believers. How sweet it is to gather together with friends and family who love you and strengthen you. How great to have a place where you can keep throwing coal on to your fire for God. My cousin planned on sending out an email of something that God is teaching her in order to ignite our fire and she asks that we throw some coal back over to her when the spirit leads. There is strength in numbers. Why not stay where the fire is?

_____

_____

_____

_____

_____

_____

_____

DAY TWO

How can you sharpen someone today? Proverbs 27:17

_____
_____
_____
_____
_____
_____
_____

DAY THREE

What strength will you bring to your friendship? Matthew 18:20

_____
_____
_____
_____
_____
_____
_____

DAY FOUR

Why is union important? Mark 3:25

_____
_____
_____
_____

_____

_____

_____

DAY FIVE

Whose arm can you hold up? Exodus 17:12

_____

_____

_____

_____

_____

_____

_____

WEEK 34/DAY ONE

Our Children

The enemy wants to torment me with concerns about my children but the Bible continually reminds me that they will return to the Lord and be His. God's Word reminds me that though they have strayed they will return to Him like the Prodigal son. This was written on September 7th. 2010. Currently, Three of my children are walking closer with the Lord and the others are is still on their way back home. God is faithful! My children will live in your presence; my descendants will be established before you Lord, in Jesus' name. Psalm 102:28 Sometimes we have to give our children over to the Lord before they will on their own look for Him and recognize Him. (Jeremiah 31:17)

_____

_____

_____

_____

_____

_____

_____

DAY TWO

Who can you pray for today that needs to return home? Luke 15: 11-32

_____

_____

_____

_____

_____

_____

DAY THREE

How much effort do you think God puts into your child's return? Luke 15:1-7

_____

_____

_____

_____

_____

_____

_____

DAY FOUR

Who loves your child most? 1 John 3:1

_____

_____

_____

_____

_____

_____

_____

DAY FIVE

Whose children will you pray for today?

_____

_____

_____

_____

_____

_____

_____

WEEK 35/DAY ONE

Storms May Come

Jesus taught by the lake. the crowd was so large that He got into a boat and taught from inside the boat. He taught them many things in parables. Among the parables He taught was one of a man who scatters seed and whether he sleeps or is awake the seed sprouts and grows and he does not know how. Mark 4:26-29. He also taught about many other things. When he was alone with his disciples He explained them.

Then, they went over to the other side (other boats went also). A storm came upon them while Jesus slept. The disciples feared and woke Him. Jesus got up and rebuked the winds and He asked his disciples, "Why are you afraid? Do you still have no faith?" Verses 35-41

As I see it, Jesus invested ample time with His disciples teaching, demonstrating, clarifying and explaining. In fact, it gives me a sense of responsibility for spiritual growth. He planted the seed but in the first trial there appeared to be no growth.

Had there been growth like the man sleeping in peace expecting his seed to grow, they too would have understood that they were traveling with the Creator and that they could have exercised their authority.

Prior to that, Jesus had already taught them about asking and seeking and He had taught them about not worrying (Matthew's account chapters 5,6,7) and He had already done many miracles in their presence. You would think that in times of distress they would recognize His power.

I have seen many miracles in my life yet in the hour of need, will I remember what He has already done?

_____

_____

_____

_____

_____

_____

DAY TWO

What miracles impact your life? Mark 5: 21-43

_____

_____

_____

_____

_____

_____

DAY THREE

What parables touch your heart? Mark 4:30-34

_____

_____

_____

_____

_____

_____

DAY FOUR

Can you walk the challenging waters of life? Matthew 14:25-33

_____

_____

_____

_____

_____

_____

DAY FIVE

What things bring you a sinking feeling? Matthew 14: 30

_____

_____

_____

_____

_____

_____

WEEK 36/DAY ONE

Choices and Decisions

Written 12/15/2010

My daughter, Priscilla, blessed me this morning with Scripture from Jeremiah 44. She showed me how the Israelites were given instructions from God but they chose not to follow it. The women were instrumental in causing the men of Israel to choose against God which brought about great wrath. The Shunammite woman, on the other hand, did everything the Prophet told her to and was blessed (2 Kings 4:8-37).

As men and women of God we have daily choices and decisions to make. Shall we choose God's way or our own. His way leads to life, while we, on the other hand, may lead ourselves to death.

When I chose a life of addictions and sin my life was coming apart. Once I chose Christ new life was birthed in me—a life that brings me daily peace even in times of hardship. The choice is ours.

_____

_____

_____

_____

_____

_____

_____

DAY TWO

The choice to obey or disobey has existed since the beginning. What's your choice? Genesis 2:15-17

_____

_____

_____

_____

_____

_____

_____

DAY THREE

Deuteronomy 30:19 Will you choose life?

_____

_____

_____

_____

_____

_____

_____

DAY FOUR

Joshua 24:15 Many may stand against you, what will you choose?

_____

_____

_____

_____

_____

_____

_____

DAY FIVE

Proverbs 14:1 Will you choose with wisdom?

_____

_____

_____

_____

_____

_____

_____

WEEK 37/DAY ONE

What I Say Matters

There are those who are relentless with their mouth. They can get angry and say whatever they feel without taking into consideration who gets hurt. I have on occasions said things that If I could I would take back. So I have learned that most often it is better to measure my words rather than to spit them out.

Here are some quotes that I have heard that have left their imprint in my life.

"Talk less, say more." (Unknown).

"I have often regretted my speech but never my silence." Syrus Publilius

"Preach the Gospel at all times. Use words if necessary." Francis Assisi.

_____

_____

_____

_____

_____

_____

_____

DAY TWO

Hebrews 11:3 What power do you think 'words' have in your everyday life?

_____

_____

_____

_____

_____

DAY THREE

Proverbs 12:6 How can words influence your life and others?

_____

_____

_____

_____

_____

DAY FOUR

Proverbs 18:21 How can you use your words to create life in someone's life?

_____

_____

_____

_____

_____

DAY FIVE

Matthew 12:36,37 How will you be held accountable for your words?

_____

_____

_____

_____

_____

_____

_____

WEEK 38/DAY ONE

He Causes Me To Smile

I stepped out of my house and into my backyard, burdened with all of the things happening around me. My best friend is experiencing a sorrowful separation from her fiancé of ten years. My son is facing a divorce from his wife of almost ten years, my daughter is scheduled for a C-Section within days, my stepson is facing a court date for a crime he committed and much more.

But God in His great mercy and love caused me to smile. In my pond were the happiest ducks I've ever seen. There were about ten to fifteen ducks just jumping and swimming and playing and diving and loving life. Nothing around them caused them fear or concern (they may not know there's an alligator in that pond). The turtles hung out on the sides of the pond without a care in the world. Above them were what sounded like hundreds of birds chirping and singing songs to one another. To my right, beautiful flowers had blossomed despite the fact that it is winter.

So, once again I am reminded that "His eye is on the sparrow and I know He watches me" and He watches mine.

_____

_____

_____

_____

_____

_____

_____

DAY TWO

Isaiah 43:2 What will you think of when you are facing a challenge?

_____

_____

_____

_____

_____

_____

_____

DAY THREE

Psalm 3:3 How can you be encouraged by this Scripture?

_____

_____

_____

_____

_____

_____

_____

DAY FOUR

2nd Chronicles 16:9a How strong is God to you?

_____

_____

_____

_____

_____

_____

_____

DAY FIVE

Deuteronomy 1:30 What can God do for you? What has He already done? Have you forgotten? Write them down.

_____

_____

_____

_____

_____

_____

_____

WEEK 39/DAY ONE

Prosperity

"A man may have a hundred children and live many years, yet no matter how long he lives, if he can't enjoy his prosperity and does not receive proper burial, I say that a still born child is better off than he." (Ecclesiastes 6:3). The writer gets personal when he tells his readers that if you have family or even friends, but cannot enjoy them, what good is it to have them? Wouldn't it be better to accept the differences between us? It is what makes us individual children of God! He goes on to say that even if you have a long life, and do not learn to enjoy what God has provided in your life, what inheritance are you leaving behind? Enjoy life; take pleasure in people; enjoy your siblings and parents and children; use those free minutes and free texts to cultivate and enhance relationships; take walks; visit people; invite friends over; be friendly to your next door neighbor. A short life lived this way is better than a long life without it, says the writer. Pastor Porfirio Thomas

_____

_____

_____

_____

_____

_____

_____

DAY TWO

1 John 1:3, 7 With whom can you fellowship with this week that you have missed lately?

_____

_____

_____

_____

_____

_____

_____

DAY THREE

Colossians 3:16 How can you encourage a family member today?

_____

_____

_____

_____

_____

_____

_____

DAY FOUR

Luke 24:13-15 How will your conversation with your friend draw Jesus near?

_____

_____

_____

_____

_____

_____

_____

<u>DAY FIVE</u>

Psalm 55:14 Will you make your home the house of the Lord and invite people in?

_____

_____

_____

_____

_____

_____

WEEK 40/DAY ONE

When I Am Down

When I am down and, oh my soul, so weary; When troubles come and my heart burdened be; Then, I am still and wait here in the silence, Until you come and sit awhile with me. You raise me up, so I can stand on mountains; You raise me up, to walk on stormy seas; I am strong, when I am on your shoulders; You raise me up . . . To more than I can be. Josh Groban

The Apostle Paul said "Do not be anxious about anything . . ." Philippians 4:6

When the car breaks down and the rent is due; when work is hard but does not pay enough, when you have a term paper to submit but haven't got enough hours in the day to complete it . . . when trouble comes . . . be still! And my God will supply all your needs according to His riches in glory in Christ Jesus. Philippians 4:19

_____
_____
_____
_____
_____
_____
_____

DAY TWO

Go to God in confidence that He will meet your need. Hebrews 4:16

_____

_____

_____

_____

_____

_____

_____

DAY THREE

Ask the Father what you need Matthew 21:22

_____

_____

_____

_____

_____

_____

_____

DAY FOUR

Get up and do good despite what you may be feeling 2 Thessalonians 3:13

_____

_____

_____

_____

_____

_____

_____

DAY FIVE

What will you do today? Psalm 37:7 James 4:8

_____

_____

_____

_____

_____

_____

WEEK 41/DAY ONE

<u>Seasons of Suffering</u>

Every now and then we find ourselves in a season of suffering. This may be that season for you. Even when we faithfully believe God and His promises, suffering will not be pleasant. Sorrow may strike, tears may become a very real part of many sleepless nights. You may feel the weight of the world on your shoulders; take heart, God is right by your side.

Meditate on this FACT: God is closer to you than your pillow is to your face when you are laying on it. He holds you safe in His tender arms. He sees each tear that runs down your face. He will not let you down.

When the season is over, if you have kept your eyes on Him, you will shine like the stars in the sky.

Rom 8:18-21: "For I consider that the sufferings of this present time are not worthy to be compared with the glory which shall be revealed in us. For the earnest expectation of the creation eagerly waits for the revealing of the sons of God." Someone said, "God will not protect us from what will perfect us."

_____

_____

_____

_____

_____

_____

_____

DAY TWO

Who do you know who is suffering right now? Please pray! Psalm 55:22

_____

_____

_____

_____

_____

_____

DAY THREE

Why do you believe God will see you through your suffering? Psalm 27:1

_____

_____

_____

_____

_____

_____

DAY FOUR

How do you know God can help you in your time of suffering? When has He helped you in the past? Hebrews 13:5

_____

_____

_____

_____

_____

_____

DAY FIVE

How will you give Him your suffering today? Psalm 55:22

_____

_____

_____

_____

_____

_____

WEEK 42/DAY ONE

Trying . . . Training . . .

"If at first you don't succeed; try, try again." Do you remember hearing this as a child? Now can you think of something you tried to do repeatedly without success? There's an inherent problem in the word, "try." To say "I'll try," leaves an "out." If I say," I'm going to try to run the New York marathon," I leave myself an out if I don't succeed. I can show up on the day of the race, run one mile, quit and then say, "well at least I tried." Trying makes failing acceptable.

In 2011 Geoffrey Mutai of Kenya broke the men's winning record when he ran the New York Marathon in two hours, five minutes and five seconds. But Geoffrey didn't just *try* to win, he trained to win. He started training at the age of 13 and eventually went on to compete and win in many races including the NY marathon at age 30.

Have you ever heard yourself say, "I'm going to try to do better," or "I'm going to try to quit lying," "try to stop gossiping," "try to have a positive attitude," "try to live righteously?" At some time or another, we have all failed at trying. Refer to I Corinthians 9:24-27 for the illustration of a runner. Just as Mutai's training program consisted of many components, our spiritual training consists of various things.

Read 2 Timothy 3:10-17 for some guidelines. We need to be around and learn from people who display the Godly traits we want to have (vs. 10 & 11). We need to persevere (vs. 14). We need to be fed by the Word of God which equips us and trains us in righteousness (vs. 16&17). We need to be disciplined, deliberate and intentional about our spiritual training. So, stop trying so hard and keep on training.

_____

_____

_____

_____

_____

_____

_____

DAY TWO

What problem area in your life have you tried to conquer without success?

_____

_____

_____

_____

_____

_____

DAY THREE

How can you apply the principles in 2 Timothy 3 to that situation?

_____

_____

_____

_____

_____

_____

_____

DAY FOUR

What specific disciplines can you put in place that would aid your "training in righteousness?"

_____

_____

_____

_____

_____

_____

DAY FIVE

Reflect on what things might be getting in the way of your giving control of your training over to the Holy Spirit.

_____

_____

_____

_____

_____

_____

WEEK 43/DAY ONE

52 Days of Thanksgiving

As was her normal routine, she perfectly blended her tempered milk and decaf Taster's Choice. Early in the morning, she sat at the head of the kitchen table, across the window, to spend her time with alone God. On the corner to her right was her "Streams in the Desert" devotional book and her worn leather bound Bible. She read as she sipped her coffee and then closed in prayer, "Thank you, Father . . . ." It was a Thursday, her day to simply give thanks.

She migrated to New York at the age of 45. This wasn't easy; she didn't speak the language, didn't know the customs and she was far from her family; yet she made this her home. She became a U.S. citizen, studying the language straight to the age of 74, learning the culture along the way. Through this she fell in love with Thanksgiving Day. She was moved by this one day of thanks, the last Thursday in November, a day to worship God by expressing our gratitude.

Years later, she developed a custom of her own, on Thanksgiving morning she would call her friend Mrs. Schaeffer, in the Dominican Republic, and together they would give thanks. How she enjoyed those blessed days; they were uniquely special. One day, the Holy Spirit moved her to make every Thursday a day of thanksgiving. On that day of the week, there would no longer be any asking, interceding, nor pleading, just thanking.

Gracias! For the rising sun and its warming rays, and for the rain which brings life; For the balanced and heavy iron that helped her earn her keep; for life and the gift of children, grandchildren and great grandchildren; for the knowledge with which God had gifted man; for all the things the Lord God had done, was doing and was about to do. Mostly, she gave thanks for the sacrifice of Jesus Christ the Son, through whom we are reconciled with our Creator, the Father.

This was one of the wise practices of my grandmother, Mamá Luz, one of God's prayer warriors. She has been gone for 18 years, but her legacy lives on in me, especially on Thursdays, the 52 days of Thanksgiving.

_____

_____

_____

_____

_____

_____

DAY TWO

Thank God for His gift of salvation and eternal life. Hebrews 12:28

_____

_____

_____

_____

_____

_____

DAY THREE

Our God is a merciful and compassionate God; how has He proven that in your life? Lamentations 3:22-23

_____

_____

_____

_____

_____

_____

_____

DAY FOUR

What special gift can you give thanks to the Lord for today? Psalm 95:2

_____

_____

_____

_____

_____

_____

_____

DAY FIVE

You too should consider using every Thursday as a day of thanksgiving . . . because His love endures forever. Psalm 136:1-9

_____

_____

_____

_____

_____

_____

_____

WEEK 44/DAY ONE

Quit Sleeping

One sunny evening, as I walked back from the river to my cabin (*the Hermitage*), I noticed a large stone wall encircling a beautiful mansion. The house and grounds were immaculate, everything within the walls was pristine, but that particular section of the wall was in shambles. It caught my attention and immediately, I was reminded of the words of the wisest man that has ever lived—King Solomon. Speaking about the vineyard of a sluggard, whose stone wall was in ruin, he said:

"A little sleep, a little slumber, a little folding of the hands to rest—and poverty will come on you like a bandit and scarcity like an armed man." (Proverbs 24:33-34)

I thought about God's children and how we sometimes neglect the walls around our spiritual vineyard. We may be playing the part of a good Christian, but not really keeping up with those things necessary to keep the spiritual bandage and armed man from dragging us down to a place of spiritual poverty.

It is my prayer that the Lord would keep me (and you) always mindful to pull all the little weeds in my life, before they take over.

_____

_____

_____

_____

_____

_____

_____

DAY TWO

Read Proverbs 24:30-34 and jot down whatever thoughts come to mind.

_____

_____

_____

_____

_____

_____

_____

DAY THREE

What is the true state of your spiritual vineyard—your relationship with God?

_____

_____

_____

_____

_____

_____

_____

DAY FOUR

What one thing, which is hindering your intimacy with God, can you begin to cut out of your life this week?

_____

_____

_____

_____

_____

_____

_____

DAY FIVE

Talk with God right now, and ask Him to help you work on what only He and you know has to be removed from your life.

_____

_____

_____

_____

_____

_____

_____

WEEK 45/DAY ONE

Fear

During a period of unemployment, I learned several lessons about fear and what it will make people do. I learned that fear will make one do things one never expected to do, that it makes us react in ways we never expected to react, say things we would never say and act in ways we never thought we could. Fear can make a person react outside of themselves—contrary to one's better judgment. In fact, when fear possesses you it can make your reasoning clouded.

Fear is lack of trust in God and His Word. If God says "don't lie" and we lie because we are afraid, what we are saying is "God, I know you said don't lie, but, I don't trust you so I have to lie or else I'll be in big trouble."

What is that? Lack of faith and often times it is our first reaction. Pray to the Father that we live lives that honor Him full of integrity so that we will be prepared to face fear and be victorious. Written 12/14/2005 **Joshua 1**

_____

_____

_____

_____

_____

_____

DAY TWO

The devil will try and stop you with fear. Fear brings many different emotions and physical changes and manifestations 2 Timothy 1:7

_____

_____

_____

_____

_____

_____

_____

DAY THREE

Make a decision "I will not fear." Romans 8:15-17

_____

_____

_____

_____

_____

_____

_____

DAY FOUR

Fear is a dead end but obedience will always overcome evil. Job 1:8

_____

_____

_____

_____

_____

_____

_____

DAY FIVE

Your can be fearful or faithful. Isaiah 41:10

_____

_____

_____

_____

_____

_____

_____

WEEK 46/DAY ONE

Growing Out Of Stagnation

"For the flesh desires what is contrary to the spirit, and the spirit what is contrary to the flesh . . ." Galatians 5:17

I recently had an experience in my life where I needed God to move. I believe in God, I trust in God. I even pray and go to church. Yet something was missing, a lack of growth and direction. It seems that I had hit a dead end or a road block at the very least. My relationship with God was stagnant like water left in a kiddy pool after summer is over. I went into my prayer closet and asked God, "How can I get out of this slump and grow?" He answered my prayer.

He revealed to me that I should fast. Fasting is a powerful tool that functions as a spiritual amplifier. It is a willful struggle to bring the flesh in tune with the spirit. These two things which are at war, when brought in line, can move your very soul. When asked by the disciples why they could not cast out an evil spirit, Jesus replied ". . . This kind comes out only by prayer and *fasting*"-Matthew 17:21.

It is very uncomfortable to fast. It can be the hardest thing to do yet be the most rewarding. God doesn't want us to be complacent or stagnant but wants you to grow.

"So because you are lukewarm, neither hot nor cold, I will spit you out of my mouth." Revelations 3:16

_____

_____

_____

_____

_____

_____

_____

DAY TWO

What areas in your life can benefit from fasting? 2 Samuel 12:16, Nehemiah 9:1-2, Daniel 9:3, Ezra 8:23

_____

_____

_____

_____

_____

_____

DAY THREE

Do I have the ability to fast? Matthew 17:20

_____

_____

_____

_____

_____

_____

DAY FOUR

Pray for strength to move out of your comfort zone and grow. Matthew 14:22-36

_____

_____

_____

_____

_____

_____

_____

DAY FIVE

How can I overcome fear of failing? 2 Timothy 1:7

_____

_____

_____

_____

_____

_____

_____

WEEK 47/DAY ONE

Tuck It In

So many women today have bought in to the perception of beauty based on the public's definition of beauty. They stretch out, they tuck in, they cut off, lift up, burn up, press down, tattoo in, suck out, added holes, greater inserts, and some would even say "I'm still not satisfied". In order to achieve the public acceptance of beauty and the acknowledgements of others. In 1Peter 3:3-6, Peter refuses the idea of establishing one's self by external beauty, while neglecting the inner beauty that only comes through the Holy Spirit and the mirror of the Word of God. He talks about an unfading beauty, a beauty of great worth in the sight of God. A beauty that takes time and discipline and the work of the Holy Spirit to attain, a gentle, quiet and submissive spirit. By all means, yes, go to the beauty parlor, fix your hair, do your nails, put on some makeup, get your extensions, look good for God and for your loved ones, but don't miss the training God has for you, that teaches you real beauty.

_____
_____
_____
_____
_____
_____
_____

DAY TWO

Esther 2:9 How will you please your king?

_____

_____

_____

_____

_____

_____

_____

DAY THREE

1 Peter 3:3-4 How would you define your internal beauty?

_____

_____

_____

_____

_____

_____

_____

DAY FOUR

What practical steps will you take to improve your internal beauty?
Proverbs 31:30

_____

_____

_____

_____

_____

_____

_____

<u>DAY FIVE</u>

Psalm 45:11 Is the King enthralled with your internal beauty?

_____

_____

_____

_____

_____

_____

_____

WEEK 48/DAY ONE

Taste and See That the Lord Is Good

God has blessed me with the privilege of travelling to several different countries, and I praise Him for these gifts. I've noticed that while some foods and drinks are similar between neighboring countries, in every country I have visited, I found tastes unique to that particular land. Once I've returned home, for a few weeks, I continue to crave those things I so enjoyed in distant places.

From the very beginning of time, God wanted us to enjoy the foods He so freely gave us. Genesis 1:29 says, "Then God said, "Behold, I have given you every plant yielding seed that is on the surface of all the earth, and every tree which has fruit yielding seed; it shall be food for you . . ." Throughout all of Scripture we find food. The Old and New Testaments are both full of details pertaining to the Feasts of the Lord and accounts centered around food. Food and drink are also used in analogies: Jesus is the Bread of Life and the Living Water; oil is symbolic of the Holy Spirit and His healing; wine is used to represent the blood of Jesus; vinegar was given to Christ while He was on the cross which causes us to think of the bitterness of His suffering. As we read God's Word, we can discover many, many instances of food and drink being mentioned, so it is obvious that it's important to our Creator, Sustainer, God.

So, then, in the first part of Psalm 34:8, the Psalmist encourages us to "taste and see that the Lord is good." Many years ago there was a television commercial for Alka Seltzer which had all of America saying, "Try it; you'll like it." Well that may very well be another way of making the Psalmist's statement; "Try God, you'll like Him." Every day the Lord proves His goodness to us . . . the ways are innumerable, but if you hadn't noticed that fact before now, try Him . . . I guarantee, you'll like Him. After "tasting," and seeing that the Lord is good, as happens to me when I return from an overseas trip, you'll be craving more of Him.

_____

_____

_____

_____

_____

_____

_____

DAY TWO

Read Acts Chapter 10 to see how God used food as a picture of how we, the Gentiles (or non-Jews), are also accepted into His Kingdom.

_____

_____

_____

_____

_____

_____

_____

DAY THREE

John 4:3-42 Have you tasted the living water today?

_____

_____

_____

_____

_____

_____

DAY FOUR

1Peter 3:18 Have you tasted milk today?

_____

_____

_____

_____

_____

_____

DAY FIVE

Matthew 4:4 Have you tasted bread today?

_____

_____

_____

_____

_____

_____

WEEK 49/DAY ONE

What Do You Smell Like?

You may have heard the Biblical account of Shadrach, Meshach and Abednego. These were three Jewish young men who were included in the people of Judah's exile to Babylon. Their story is noteworthy because of their faithfulness to the One True God. They refused to bow to King Nebuchadnezzar so they were served with a death sentence, and were thrown into a fiery furnace. The result of their faithfulness to God was that they were kept alive, while the soldiers who threw them into the furnace were instantly killed because of the extreme heat of the flames. This account is so wonderful; you should take some time to read the whole story found in the third chapter of Daniel.

I would like to call your attention the 27th verse, "The satraps, the prefects, the governors and the king's high officials gathered around and saw in regard to these men that the fire had no effect on the bodies of these men nor was the hair of their head singed, nor were their trousers damaged, nor had the smell of fire even come upon them." What I want you to pay close attention to is the last part of that verse, "nor had the smell of fire even come upon them." These young men did not smell of the fire that threatened to consume them. This causes me to think about the fact that our spiritual scent is so important.

2 Corinthians 2:14-15 says, "But thanks be to God, who always leads us as captives in Christ's triumphal procession and uses us to spread the aroma of the knowledge of Him everywhere. For we are to God

the pleasing aroma of Christ among those who are being saved . . ." So, then . . . as we go through the spiritual fires that could cause us to come out smelling foul, let's remember that, no matter what, to God we are the pleasing aroma of Christ. If we are the pleasing aroma of Christ, how shall we spread this wonderful fragrance?

Through prayer. Psalm 141:2a

_____

_____

_____

_____

_____

_____

_____

DAY TWO

By loving others. Ephesians 5:2

_____

_____

_____

_____

_____

_____

_____

DAY THREE

By spreading God's Word. 2 Corinthians 2:14

_____

_____

_____

_____

_____

_____

_____

DAY FOUR

By providing for the needs of others (especially those serving the Lord). Philippians 4:18

_____

_____

_____

_____

_____

_____

_____

DAY FIVE

Through our tithes and offerings. Leviticus 1:1,2

_____

_____

_____

_____

_____

_____

_____

WEEK 50/DAY ONE

<u>He Touched Me</u>

"And it came about that while He was in one of the cities, behold, there was a man full of leprosy; and when he saw Jesus, he fell on his face and implored Him, saying, "Lord if You are willing, You can make me clean." And he stretched out His hand, and touched him, saying, "I am willing; be cleansed." And immediately the leprosy left him."

I find this Scripture so captivating . . . you see . . . in Jesus' day, people with leprosy had to live very far away from anyone. From the time leprosy touched their bodies, they had to live out the rest of their existence away from any other human being who did not have this disease. If they were going to be near healthy people, they had to yell loudly to let everyone know that a leper was near. But in this account, we see that one of them had the audacity . . . yes, it took audacity . . . to go to Jesus, fall on his face, and implore of Him to make him clean. He did something very interesting; he expressed Jesus' authority over illness, by saying, ". . . if You are willing." In other words, He understood that Jesus had the power to "will" him whole. Then, Jesus . . . full of compassion . . . expressed His willingness and He ***touched him***. He could have simply said the words and the man would have been healed. He didn't have to touch him, but He did. I believe that by touching this leper, Jesus spoke louder than any words could have. The healing touch of Jesus made the leper whole, and it can also make us whole today.

Whatever your circumstance today, have the audacity to call on Jesus and ask Him to touch you . . . He will.

_____

_____

_____

_____

_____

_____

_____

DAY TWO

Matthew 8:2-4, 14-16, 17:6-8 Why will you allow Jesus to touch you?

_____

_____

_____

_____

_____

_____

_____

DAY THREE

Matthew 9:28-30, Matthew 20:34 How will you allow Jesus to touch you?

_____

_____

_____

_____

_____

_____

_____

DAY FOUR

Luke 7:14 & 22:50-52 Where will you allow Jesus to touch you?

_____
_____
_____
_____
_____
_____
_____

DAY FIVE

Mark 1:40-42 & 7:32-34 When will you allow Jesus to touch you? NOW?

_____
_____
_____
_____
_____
_____
_____

WEEK 51/DAY ONE

He Who Has Ears

The sense of hearing is in use constantly; However, we do not take it into account or notice that it is being used constantly and actively. The skill to hear sounds, voices, music, birds, animals, insects, telephones, televisions, etc., is incredible! All too often, we do not acknowledge the skill that we have of being able to hear all the time, but occasionally we stop us to listen to, and we are captivated by listening to the sounds of life that surrounds us. Sounds like the breeze, the drops of rain, the whisper of electrical appliances, a train in the distance, cars passing, waves, kisses, breathing, and so much more.

I looked up the meaning of the word, "hear" and I came across the following; "Perceived sound through the ear, Pay attention to what is being said, Listen to." After reading this definition, I immediately remembered the words that Jesus said many times, "he who has ears to hear, let him hear." These words have always intrigued me, but possibly for the first time, now I am delving more to achieve a better understanding of what these words of our Lord truly mean.

Generally, when we study the Bible, it is good to notice when something is repeated. That is the case with this phrase; These same words are found 15 times in the New Testament (see the notes of Biblical references). Although the occasions in which Jesus says these words are different, I think that the lesson is always the same. Having ears to hear means that we understand what God requires of us. It seems that Jesus is saying, "pay attention, this is not optional!"

Although the sense of natural hearing is extraordinary, Christians have an incredible gift for spiritual hearing through faith in Jesus Christ! The ability to hear what God says is exceptional! The word of God is given to us so that we can "hear" the voice of God and know what His will is. Matthew 24: 15 says, "he who reads, understands."

Someone has said that, "God rarely raises the voice." Are you listening carefully?

_____
_____
_____
_____
_____
_____

DAY TWO

What is God telling to you? Matthew 13: 9

_____
_____
_____
_____
_____
_____

DAY THREE

Are you doing what you are listening to? Mark 4: 9, 23

_____

_____

_____

_____

_____

_____

DAY FOUR

What does Jesus want us to listen to and understand? Mark 7:14

_____

_____

_____

_____

_____

_____

DAY FIVE

What did Jesus want His disciples to hear? Luke 8:8 & 11-15

_____

_____

_____

_____

_____

_____

_____

WEEK 52/DAY ONE

Remember

I stop in the midst of my day to sit and contemplate the wondrous creation of God. I see the trees and the flowers and the birds that He created and am amazed at His awesomeness. I watch as the ant carries her meal and precisely calculates its weight to determine whether help will be required. I listen to the chirp of the birds and watch as they carefully craft their nest and prepare for their young. A lizard crosses my feet and knows enough to move quickly to avoid danger and a bumble bee seeks diligently for flowers from whence her honey will come.

Yet I stumble upon my own disbelief and am perplexed at how often I miss seeing God's glory and how quickly I forget His wonder and how soon I neglect to remember how He saved me yesterday and the day before and the day before. I run quickly in fear of how I will resolve this or that problem and do not remember that God saved me from that situation a short while ago. Why do I forget so easily? Why does it take such effort to keep my focus and trust Him in all things. 1 Chronicles 16:12 says "Remember the wonders He has done . . ." later verse 15 says, "He remembers His covenant forever . . ."

I want to always remember, so I write my thoughts, my experiences and look to them every so often so that when I tend to forget I can remember. He is perfect and He never forgets.

_____
_____
_____
_____
_____
_____
_____

DAY TWO

Deuteronomy 8: 2 How's your memory?

_____
_____
_____
_____
_____
_____

DAY THREE

Deuteronomy 8: 18 Do you remember when . . ?

_____
_____
_____
_____
_____
_____

DAY FOUR

Exodus 20:8 Have you remembered to rest lately?

_____

_____

_____

_____

_____

_____

_____

DAY FIVE

Isaiah 38:3 What is God's remembrance of you?

_____

_____

_____

_____

_____

_____

_____

About the Author

Ephesians 2:1-10 sums up my story. Although I woke up every day with breath in my lungs, my heart beating, my mind thinking, my eyes seeing, my mouth speaking and most of my body functioning normally I lived as if I were dead. I made poor decisions daily which carried with them severe consequences. I polluted my body with drugs and allowed misconduct to be a part of my daily routine. While surrounded by friends and activities I could function, once in the sole presence of my thoughts I was dying. I really had no life. The drugs were not sufficient, my beloved husband was not enough, my children could not fill my void, my friends didn't count; I was alone and dying. But for God's great love I would have perished!

God has made me alive with Christ in order that He may show m the incomparable riches of His Grace. He has given me life; and life to do good works that others may be saved.

Balderes Lucila Santos de Alvarez

VITA

Balderes Lucila Santos de Alvarez
AKA Lucy

October 9, 1958	Born—Santo Domingo, Rep. Dom.
1986	Ordained as a Minister
1998	B.S., Nyack College
2009	B.S., Faith Theological College
2012	Master., Faith Theological College

The Ministry of "Diamonds In The Rough Unveiled" is Spiritually and Prayerfully supported by All Souls Crossroad Church whose leaders are Pastor Porfirio Thomas and Graciela Thomas and inspired by my daughter, Melody Nicole Cruz.

Melody Nicole Cruz.